Simone Biles
A Little Golden Book® Biography

By JaNay Brown-Wood
Illustrated by Kim Holt

A GOLDEN BOOK • NEW YORK

Text copyright © 2023 by JaNay Brown-Wood
Cover art and interior illustrations copyright © 2023 by Kim Holt
All rights reserved. Published in the United States by Golden Books, an imprint of Random House Children's Books, a division of Penguin Random House LLC, 1745 Broadway, New York, NY 10019. Golden Books, A Golden Book, A Little Golden Book, the G colophon, and the distinctive gold spine are registered trademarks of Penguin Random House LLC.
rhcbooks.com
Educators and librarians, for a variety of teaching tools, visit us at RHTeachersLibrarians.com
Library of Congress Control Number: 2022931980
ISBN 978-0-593-56673-2 (trade) — ISBN 978-0-593-56674-9 (ebook)

Printed in the United States of America
10 9 8

Simone Arianne Biles was born on March 14, 1997, in Columbus, Ohio. She lived with her mother and two older siblings, Ashley and Tevin. When she was two years old, her little sister, Adria, was born.

Unfortunately, her mother couldn't care for them. After some time in a foster home, Simone's older siblings went to live with their great-aunt. Simone and Adria were adopted by their grandparents, Ronald and Nellie. They raised the girls in Spring, Texas, as if they were their own children.

Simone's parents noticed that she had a lot of energy and very little fear. She would do flips and tumbles around the house, in the backyard, and even off the mailbox!

Doctors diagnosed Simone with Attention Deficit/Hyperactivity Disorder (ADHD). That explained why she was so physically active and often had a hard time focusing.

When Simone was six years old, she went on a field trip to a gymnastics center. While she was there, Simone copied the moves of the gymnasts. Her natural talent caught the eye of a coach, who asked Simone's parents to sign her up for gymnastics classes—and they did!

Gymnastics presented an ideal fit for Simone and her high energy. She flipped with power and ease on the floor, balance beam, and vault. The uneven bars were more challenging for her. But she kept at it, trying to perfect her moves.

Simone practiced almost every day. She knew that hard work and discipline were necessary for her to be her best. At just ten years old, she was competing against top gymnasts from across the country.

When she was thirteen, Simone started homeschooling. This allowed her to learn and study while sticking to her busy training schedule.

At fourteen, Simone tried for a spot on the United States women's national gymnastics team. She just missed making it, but she didn't give up. She worked even harder—and made the team the very next year!

In 2013, at the age of sixteen, Simone became the first African American to win the world all-around title. She went on to win that title in 2014 and 2015 as well, making her the first female gymnast to win the world all-around title three years in a row!

What did Simone do next?

She went to the Olympics! Simone competed in Rio de Janeiro, Brazil, in 2016, and made Olympic history by becoming the first US gymnast to win four gold medals. (She also won one bronze.) And she was named the Olympic all-around champion!

Simone was the smallest US Olympian at the Rio Games, but her amazing performance was big news. Team USA chose her to carry the American flag at the closing ceremony. The flag towered over the 4-foot, 8-inch Olympian, but she carried it with grace and pride!

Afterward, Simone and her teammates traveled around the US doing gymnastics routines in front of sold-out crowds. They performed in more than thirty states and met lots of adoring fans.

Not only has Simone performed difficult moves, but she has also created new ones! There are four moves named after her—two for the floor, one for the balance beam, and one for the vault.

It takes a lot of discipline to become a world-class gymnast like Simone. In addition to the long hours of practicing and exercising, Simone makes sure to eat healthy foods every day. But after a competition, she treats herself to pepperoni pizza!

When Simone does take a break from training, she loves to shop, hang out with her friends, play games with her family, and travel. Her favorite place to go is Belize.

Simone has faced some hard times during her career. She has spoken out about abuse she experienced at the hands of a doctor who worked with the US women's national gymnastics team.

At the 2018 US Gymnastics Championships—where she won her fifth all-around title—Simone wore a teal leotard to show her support for all those who had been abused.

In 2019, while Simone was training for the next Olympics, a global pandemic broke out. Because so many people were getting sick with the COVID-19 virus, the 2020 Olympics were postponed. This was upsetting for many of the athletes. They had worked so hard to be ready to compete.

The 2020 Olympic Games finally took place in 2021, in Tokyo, Japan. Simone was expected to be in six events, but she decided to compete in just one.

disappointed. But Simone was brave for listening to her body. She knew she had to take care of herself. "Mental health comes first," she said. "That's more important than any other medal you could win."

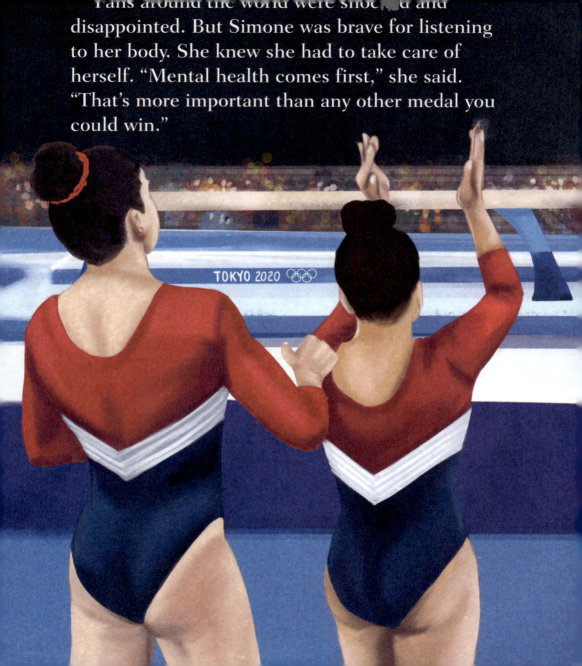

Simone stayed in Tokyo and cheered her teammates on. In the end, she won the bronze medal in the balance beam event and a silver team medal.

Simone is considered to be the greatest gymnast of all time. She has won more Olympic and World Championship medals than any other gymnast. She has spoken courageously about ADHD, stopping abuse, and the importance of mental health. And in 2022, President Biden awarded her the Presidential Medal of Freedom. Simone Biles is a perfect example that powerful things can come in small packages!